BIRDS

by Jane Werner Watson
pictures by Eloise Wilkin

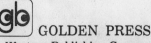
GOLDEN PRESS
Western Publishing Company, Inc.
Racine, Wisconsin

In this first book, a sense of the joy and wonder of birds is created for every child through Eloise Wilkin's sensitive illustrations and Jane Werner Watson's informative text. The songbirds in the trees, the waders of seashore and river, pigeons and chickens —over twenty birds have been simply described and vividly pictured in a way that every child will enjoy.

Sixth Printing, 1975

Canada Geese

Birds can fly.
They fly high.
Some fly miles across the sky.

Purple Martins

In the spring birds build nests. Not to rest in.
They build nests for their eggs, for their young.

Some birds bring twigs and leaves, bits of string.
What a nest!

Robins

Day and night mother bird
and father bird watch their eggs.
They keep them safe and warm. *Wood Thrushes*

Soon *chip chip* the eggs crack.
And out slip baby birds.

Mockingbirds

They have no feathers. They cannot fly.
But they are hungry. They can eat. Oh my!

Red-winged Blackbirds

Bluebirds

What do the babies eat?
Worms and grubs,
beetles and bugs
and tiny insect eggs.

Scarlet Tanager

They can eat ever so much—
caterpillars, grasshoppers, ants and
flies and such.

Soon the young birds grow feathers.
They have lessons to learn.
They must learn to mind Mother,
and to find their food.

Quail

Some take a turn at learning to swim.

Mallard Ducks

And most birds learn to fly.

Towhees

Some birds fly far. Some fly so far we cannot see how they find their way. For they fly hundreds of miles through pathless sky.

Plovers

Tree Swallows

Some birds catch their food as they fly. They snap up moths and other insects going by. They have beaks that can snap shut fast.

Many birds like grain and seeds.

Chickens, Pigeons

They have short, sharp bills for pecking. They crack seeds open or swallow foods whole.

Fruits and berries are the foods some birds need. They swallow the berries. Then they scatter the seeds.

Rose-breasted Grosbeak

Cedar Waxwing

Goldfinch

Summer passes. Weeds and grasses fade.
Fruits disappear.

Cold winds shake the trees and bushes.
Winter time is near.

Warbler

Something tells the birds to fly southward.
Off in flocks they go.

Heron

Larks and warblers, thrushes, thrashers,
gray geese following their leaders—
off they fly with a honk or a cry.

Thrasher

Horned Lark

Chickadees

Woodpecker

Nuthatch

Some birds stay.
Bread and suet and seeds are the food
a bird needs in the cold.
On the snow you may see
a small chickadee hunting seeds.

Wren

The spring will bring back many birds
to sing.
They will nest, raise their broods,
hunt their foods, sometimes rest.
The right time for each they know best.